...covering Allah

A Collection of Quranic Verses and Sayings from the 14 Ma'soomeen

When we think about Allāh, it should be with an outlook of love, honor, mercy, and compassion. After all, He is involved and helps us in all our affairs. One way that we can strengthen our remembrance of Allāh is by looking at and appreciating His blessings. By doing so, we are able to see Allāh in everything and everywhere.

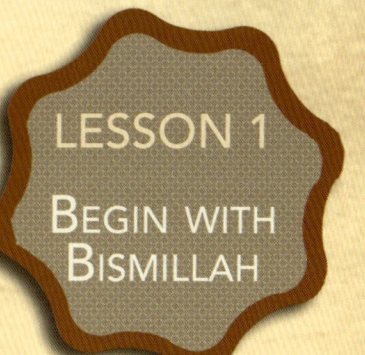

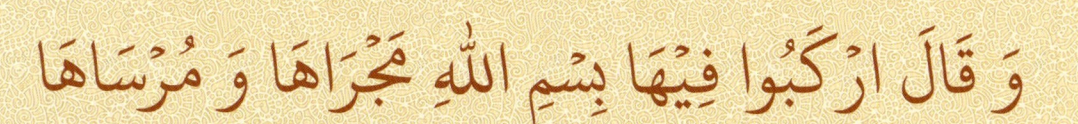

And he [Prophet Nuh] said [to the travellers], "Board it [the ark] with the Name of Allah, and it shall set sail and cast anchor."

Sūrah Hūd, Verse 41

One day, Prophet Muhammad (s) was walking down the street when he came across Shaytaan. When he looked more closely, he noticed that Shaytaan seemed very weak and tired, so he asked him, "How did you get so weak?"

Shaytaan angrily answered, "I'm suffering nonstop pain and torture from your Muslims!"

The Prophet (s) curiously asked, "Why? What have they done to you? How are they bothering you?"

"Well," replied Shaytaan, "They have seven habits that really annoy me:

1) When they begin any action, they say 'Bismillahir Rahmanir Raheem' (In the name of Allah, the Most Kind, the Most Merciful).
2) When they meet, they greet each other by saying 'Salaamun Alaikum' (Peace be upon you).
3) When they first see each other, they shake hands.
4) Whenever they plan to do something, they say 'inshaAllah' (only if Allah wants it to happen).
5) They always ask each other for forgiveness. (This one ruins all of my hard work!)
6) Whenever they hear your name, they recite a *Salawaat* and send blessings upon you!
7) They follow your Ahlul Bayt (a) and are kind to their followers."

Anwār ul-Majālis, Ch. 5, Vol. 88

لَوْ قَرَأْتَ بِسْمِ اللهِ تَحْفَظُكَ الْمَلَائِكَةُ إِلَى الْجَنَّةِ

Prophet Muhammad (s):
If you say "Bismillah" [before starting anything], the angels will protect you all the way until you reach Heaven.

Fiqh ar-Ridā(a), P. 342

LESSON 2
Always Remember Allah

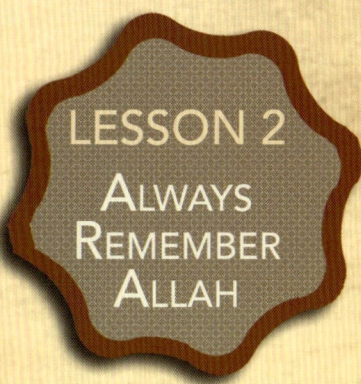

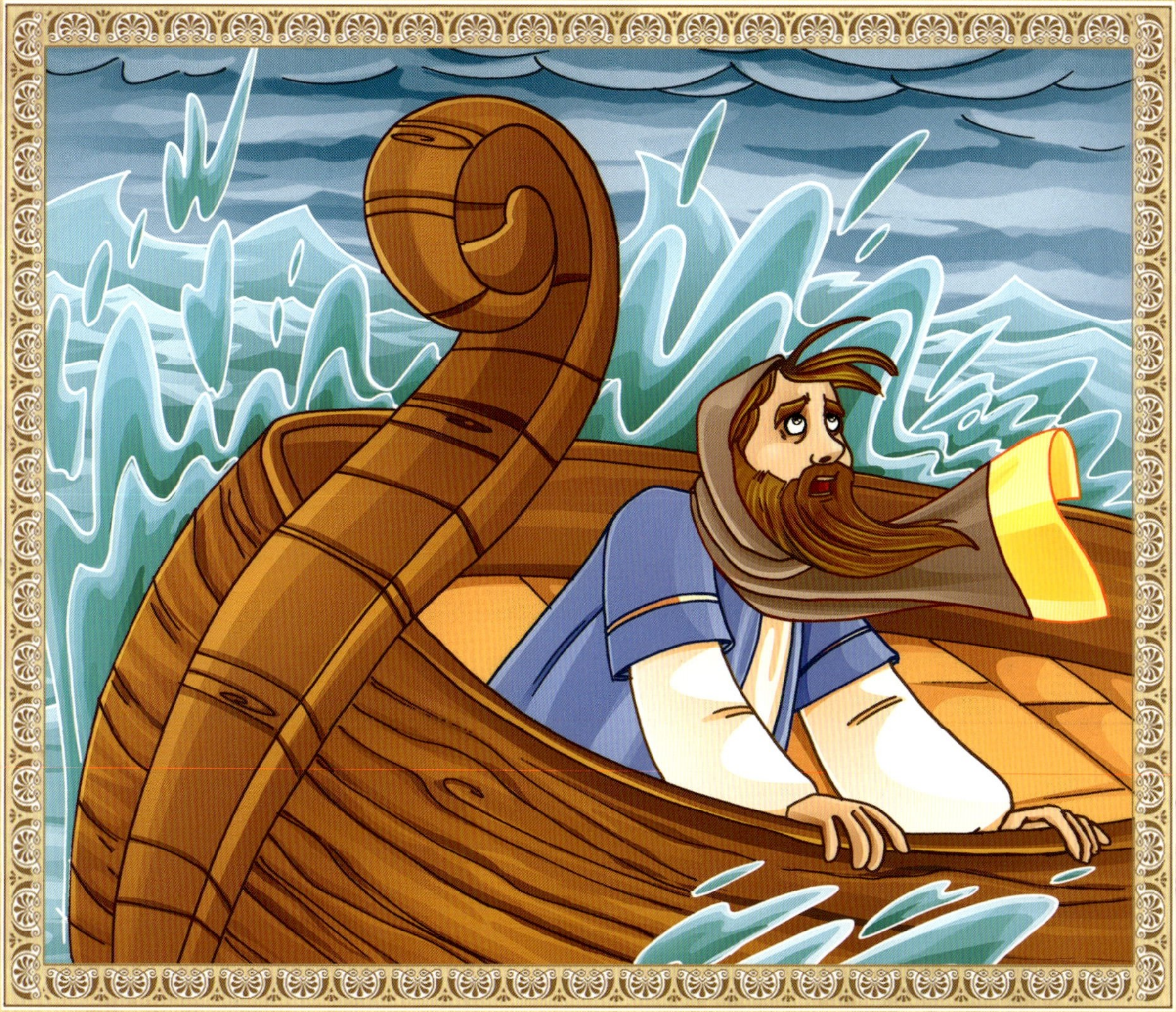

فَاذْكُرُونِي أَذْكُرْكُمْ

Remember Me, and I will remember you.

Sūrah al-Baqarah, Verse 152

There was once a man who had an important question. He tried to find the answer to his question, but nobody could help him! Finally, he decided to visit Imam Sadiq (a). After all, he heard that the Imam (a) was the wisest and smartest of all.

The next day, when he met with the Imam (a), he was bursting to ask his question. After greeting the Imam (a), he took a deep breath and asked, "If we can't see Allah, how do we know that He is there?"

The Imam (a) paused for a moment. Instead of giving him a quick answer, he asked the man, "Have you ever been on a boat in the middle of the sea?"

The man nodded his head, remembering the time he sailed through the Red Sea.

"And was there ever a strong and sudden storm that ruined your boat until it started to sink?" continued the Imam (a).

"Yes! That happened to me before," the man said quickly, wondering how the Imam (a) knew about that time when he almost drowned in the sea.

The Imam (a) went on, "When you think back to that moment when you were so scared and alone, and there was nobody around to help you or save you, didn't you still have hope that you would be saved?"

"Yes, deep down inside, I still had hope!" the man admitted.

"So, who did you think was going to save you?" asked the Imam (a). The man was speechless.

"At that moment, you had hope in Allah," said the Imam (a). "You knew that only Allah could save you when nothing else could."

The man felt so relieved and finally understood Allah better! He thanked the Imam (a) for helping him realize something so important. Now that he was sure that Allah is always there, he was able to think about Allah and pray so much more and better than before!

Biḥār ul-Anwār, Vol. 3, P. 41

مَنْ أَكْثَرَ ذِكْرَ اللهِ أَحَبَّهُ اللهُ

Prophet Muhammad (s):
Allah loves those who always remember Him.

Al-Kāfī, Vol. 2, P. 499

Lesson 3
Ask Allah for Health

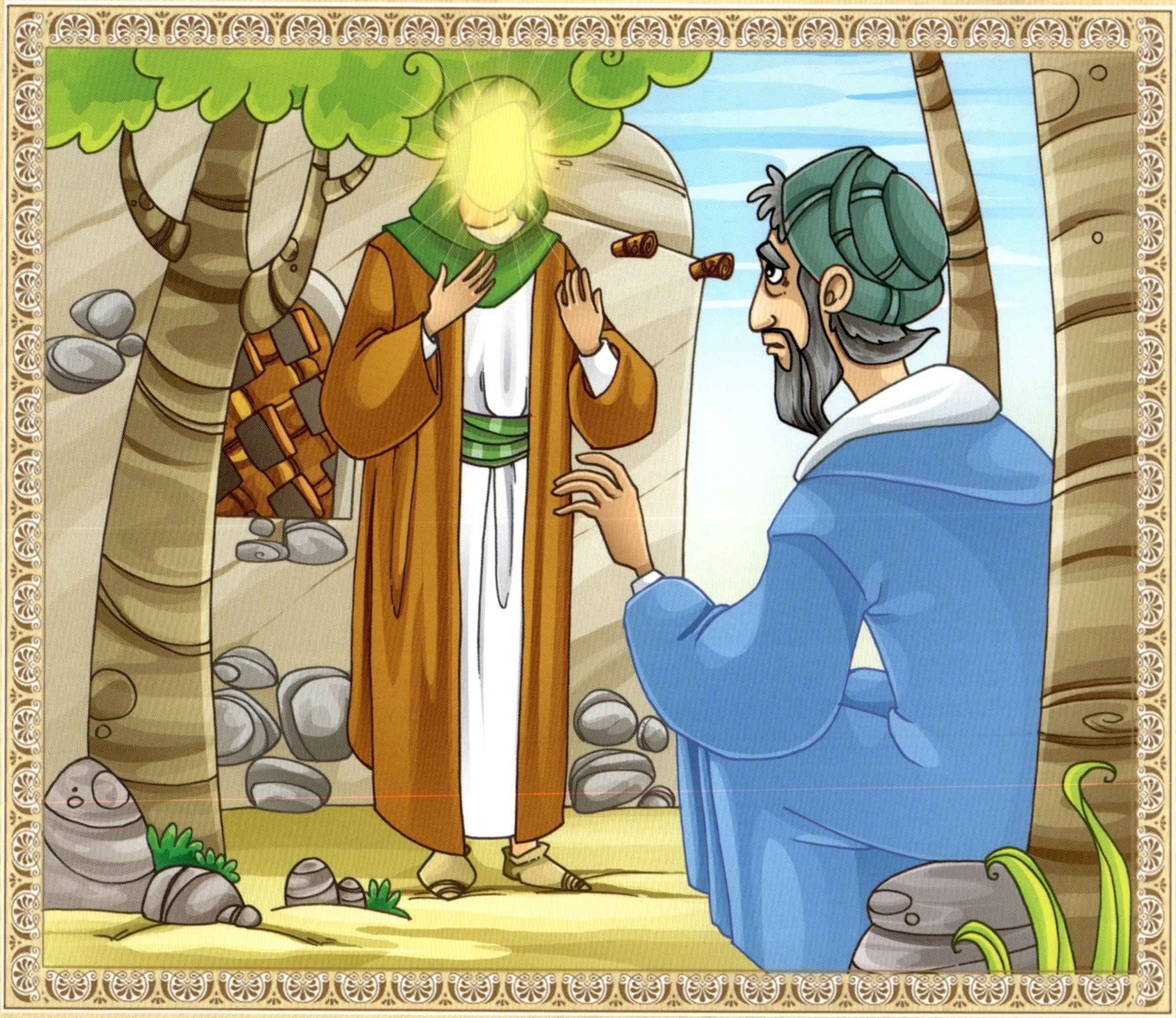

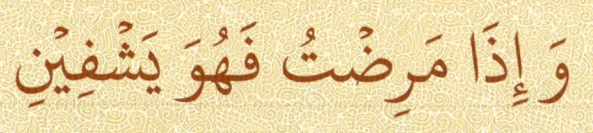

وَإِذَا مَرِضْتُ فَهُوَ يَشْفِينِ

And when I get sick, it is [Allah] who cures me.

Sūrah ash-Shuʿarāʾ, Verse 80

In a town in Iraq there lived a man who was very sick. Night and day, he was always in pain. After seeing one doctor after the other, and trying one medicine after another, he was not feeling any better. Nothing cured him!

Just as he was feeling hopeless, one of his friends said, "Why don't you go to Imam Hadi (a) and ask him to pray for you? Don't you know that the Imam's prayers are accepted?" He decided to take his friend's advice and a a few days later, he was on his way to visit the Imam (a).

The moment the man saw the Imam (a), he stopped in his tracks. He did not have the courage to ask the Imam (a) for his prayers. Before he could say anything, the Imam (a) broke the silence, "May Allah grant you health, may Allah grant you health, may Allah grant you health!" The man was shocked and speechless. *How did he know?* he thought to himself.

One man was standing nearby and saw the whole thing. "SubhaanAllah!" he exclaimed happily. "You'll feel better very soon. Our Imam (a) prayed for your health before you could even ask him!"

For a moment, the sick man felt like he was dreaming. He walked back home feeling so thankful to Allah. The next morning, he jumped out of bed with bursting energy! He had never felt better!

Biḥār ul-Anwār, Vol. 50, P. 145

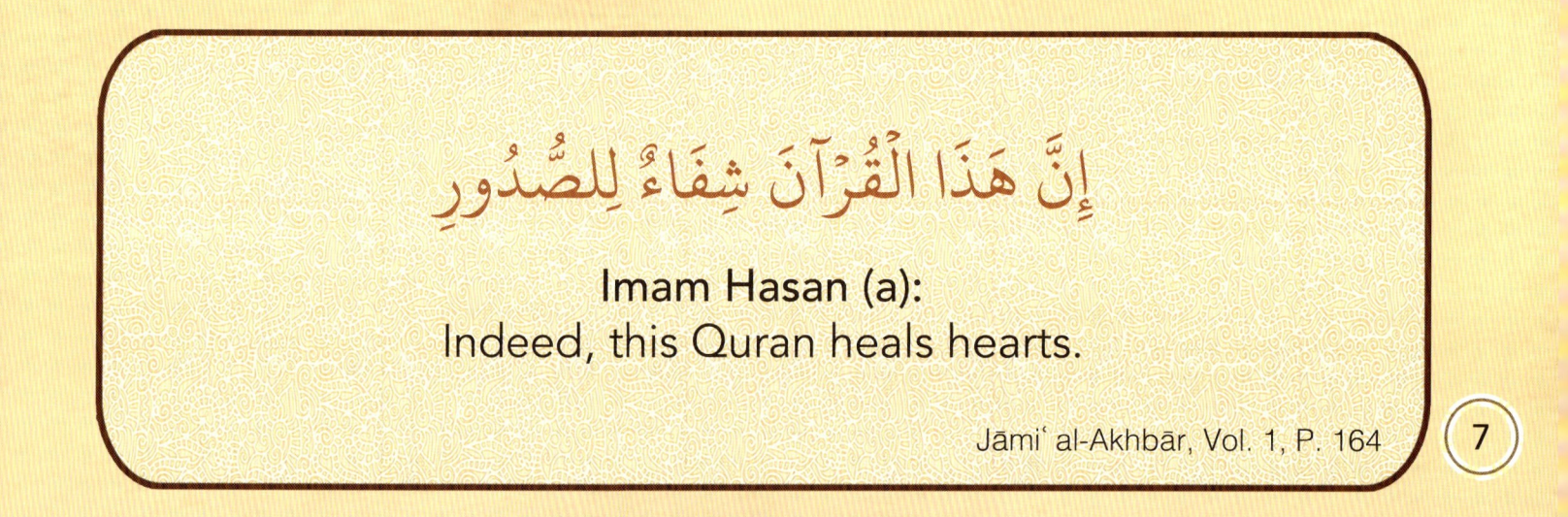

إِنَّ هَذَا الْقُرْآنَ شِفَاءٌ لِلصُّدُورِ

Imam Hasan (a):
Indeed, this Quran heals hearts.

Jāmiʿ al-Akhbār, Vol. 1, P. 164

أَلَمْ يَعْلَمْ بِأَنَّ اللّٰهَ يَرَىٰ

Does he not know that Allah sees (everything)?

Sūrah al-'Alaq, Verse 14

Abdullah was a pious man who owned a big orchard full of fruit. Every time he picked the fruit from his trees, he would donate some of it to the poor and needy. In return for his kindness and generosity, the poor people decided to help him take care of the orchard. Abdullah was very thankful to them for their help.

As the years passed, he grew older and weaker. One day, after he had fallen very sick, he advised his children, "My dear sons, please continue to give fruit to the poor and needy, especially those who work in the orchard. You should always share what you have with others." The three sons promised their father that they would take his advice.

But soon after Abdullah passed away, they broke their promise. They were too greedy and wanted all of the fruit for themselves. So, they decided to go to the orchard early in the morning to pick all of the fruit while everyone was still asleep. When the poor workers found this out, they realized that the three sons were being very greedy. For this reason, they decided that they would no longer help out at the orchard.

Soon enough, the orchard became very messy, and the trees were not growing as well anymore. The oldest brother looked at the orchard and thought, *the orchard looks much worse now!* This made him realize that what they were doing was wrong!

With his father's advice in mind, he told his two brothers, "Let's help the poor. We need to remember Allah, for He can see everything that we do." But no matter how much he tried to warn them, his brothers did not listen. They continued picking the fruit early in the morning, before the others came.

One stormy night, lightning struck one of the trees, setting it on fire! The next morning, as they approached the orchard, they saw that the entire orchard and all the fruit had been burned down! When the oldest son saw this, he said to his brothers, "This is all your fault! If you did not forget Allah, this would never have happened!" Seeing this, the two brothers realized their mistake and immediately asked Allah for forgiveness.

Tafsīr an-Namūnah, Vol. 24, P. 394

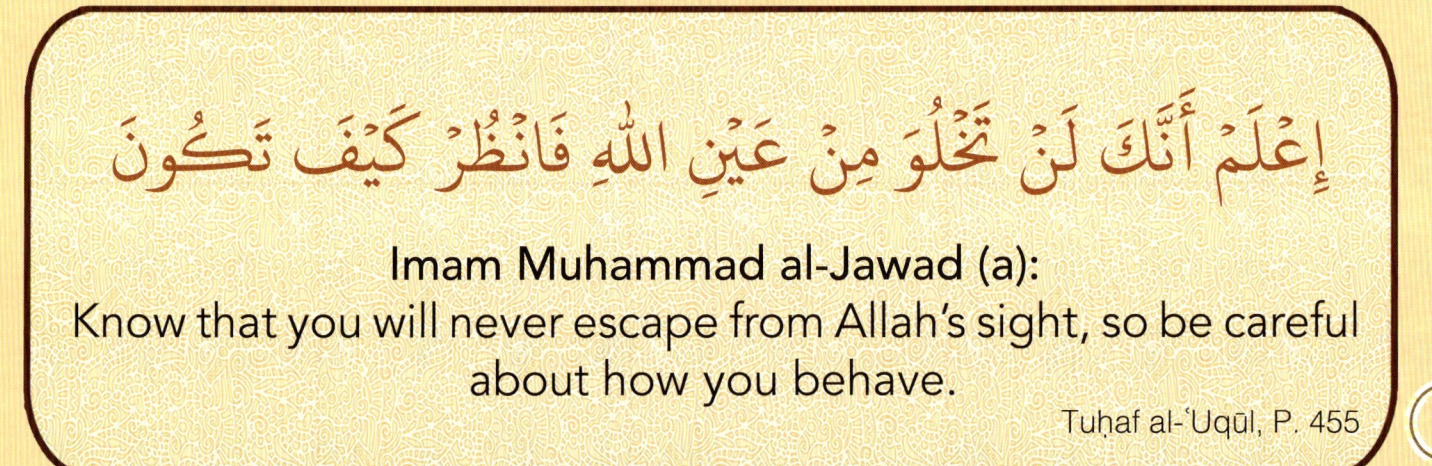

إِعْلَمْ أَنَّكَ لَنْ تَخْلُوَ مِنْ عَيْنِ اللهِ فَانْظُرْ كَيْفَ تَكُونَ

Imam Muhammad al-Jawad (a):
Know that you will never escape from Allah's sight, so be careful about how you behave.

Ṭuḥaf al-ʿUqūl, P. 455

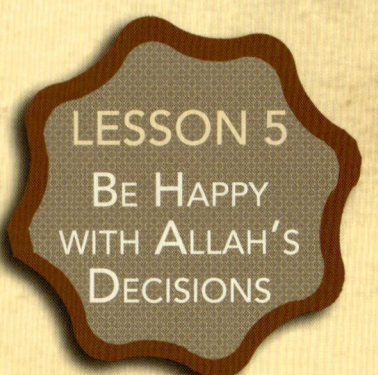

وَ اللّٰهُ يَعْلَمُ وَأَنْتُمْ لَا تَعْلَمُونَ

And Allah knows what you do not know.

Sūrah al-Baqarah, Verse 216

There was once a man who had two daughters. His first daughter was married to a farmer, and his second daughter was married to a potter.

One day, he decided to visit both of his daughters. When he went to visit his first daughter, she was thrilled to see him! She gently asked, "Dearest Father, may I ask you for a favor? This year, my husband planted many seeds in our farm. Please pray that it rains a lot so that we can have good crops!" The father smiled and said, "inshaAllah." After having some tea and biscuits, he said goodbye and made his way to his second daughter's house.

When he arrived, his second daughter was also very happy to see him. She said to him, "My dear Father, may I ask you for a favor? My husband spent the whole year making many beautiful clay dishes. Please pray that it does not rain! If it rains, the dishes won't dry fast enough and we won't be able to sell them." Once again, the father smiled and said, "inshaAllah." After having some juice and cookies, he said goodbye and headed home.

On his way back, he thought deeply about what had happened. Both of his daughters had asked him to make a prayer, but the two prayers were the opposite of each other. Since the man was wise and pious, he prayed to Allah, "O Allah, we don't know what is best for us, so please do whatever You think is best, because You know everything."

Biḥār ul-Anwār, Vol. 4

اِرْضَ تَسْتَرِحْ

Imam Ali (a):
Be content (with what you have), and you will be at peace.

QUIZ YOURSELF!

1. Shaytaan gets weaker when we _____. (Circle all that apply.)
   a. start every action with *Bismillah*
   b. greet each other with *Salaamun Alaikum*
   c. share food with others

2. In the Quran, Allah promises us that if we remember Him, He will _____.
   a. reward us
   b. take us to Heaven
   c. remember us

3. Imam Hasan (a) has told us that _____ heals our hearts.
   a. prayer
   b. the Quran
   c. medicine

4. Imam Jawad (a) warns us to be careful because _____.
   a. Allah sees everything we do
   b. the world is dangerous
   c. we might get hurt

5. We should always be _____ with Allah's decisions because He knows what's best for us.
   a. confused
   b. angry
   c. satisfied

6. Name two lessons that you learned from this book.

EMAIL YOUR ANSWERS TO QUIZZES@KISAKIDS.ORG, AND WE WILL SEND YOU A CERTIFICATE!